NEW ZEALAND'S

SOUTH ISLAND

—•— • IN COLOUR •—•—

NEW ZEALAND'S
SOUTH ISLAND
—•IN COLOUR•—

PHOTOGRAPHS: MARTIN BARRIBALL
TEXT: MERVYN DYKES

REED

Published by Reed Books,
a division of Reed Publishing (NZ) Ltd,
39 Rawene Road, Birkenhead, Auckland. Associated companies,
branches and representatives throughout the world.

ISBN 7900 0375 9

First published 1982
Reprinted 1986, 1987, 1989, 1992
This edition 1994

Cover design by Susan Johnson
Typeset by Jacobsons Graphic Communications
Printed in Hong Kong

Introduction

Maui, the Maori hero of legend, is said to have hauled the North Island of New Zealand from the sea. For this purpose he needed a sturdy canoe, which he found in the larger and geologically older South Island. By all systems of measurement it is a most remarkable vessel.

The South Island, and Stewart Island at its foot, together cover some 15,150 hectares — not a large area by world standards, but embracing an incredible variety of scenery, some with a beauty that defies description.

Easily the most striking feature is the serrated mountain spine, the Southern Alps, which divides the island into two longitudinally. However, there are other distinct regions that make equally important separate contributions to the marvellous whole: in the north are the sunshine-rich market gardens and beaches of Nelson and Marlborough; down the eastern side of the alps run the fertile alluvial Canterbury Plains; and across the divide is the raw, craggy West Coast, which is still a frontier today. The south-west of the South Island is known as Fiordland. Words cannot describe adequately its incredible beauty, which seems to have the power to touch hearts and change lives. And to the south-east lie the twin provinces of Otago and Southland.

From 1861 men flocked to Otago from all over the world in search of gold. They were hard, hopeful men, some fired by greed but others wanting no more than the chance of a new life in a new land. Into this second category fell the settlers, many of whom came to New Zealand in large groups as part of regional colonisation programmes. They made the most lasting contributions of all who came. Whereas the miners took what they wanted and left, the settlers were soon engaged in a longer struggle against daunting odds.

Patterns emerged in settlement, too. Christchurch today retains its strong English influence, with evidence of a few Scottish threads running through. At Akaroa on Banks Peninsula there is a pocket of French influence, which residents are proud to maintain. Dunedin in the deep south is staunchly Scottish and boasts its own six-metre statue of Robbie Burns.

The South Island set much of the early pace for development in New Zealand. Rich gold finds fuelled industrial development in Dunedin to the extent that, for many years, it was the country's leading manufacturing and commercial centre. Here also New Zealand's first university was established, and Dunedin's rich brought in treasures from many parts of the world to grace their homes.

Today the South Island is a victim of a population drift to the north. In 1982 about 70 per cent of New Zealand's population lives in the North Island, with the biggest concentration centred on Auckland. Attempts are being made to redress the balance by bringing heavy industry back to the south, but the north continues to grow at a faster rate.

Perhaps the scales will turn naturally when residents of the more crowded northern cities look south and see what has been left behind. Wide-open spaces, frontiers and unspoiled places are still there for all who seek them. There are fine bathing beaches and fruitful fishing grounds. Rich market gardens, orchards and vineyards have their places in the south, and forests, wild rivers, waterfalls and hot pools can be found there, too.

The bigger cities have jealously hung on to trees, gardens and waterways. Wherever possible these have been kept carefully maintained so there is always a retreat from the oppressiveness of the concrete jungle.

But, above all, the mountains reign supreme. Less than 25 per cent of New Zealand's surface is under 200 metres above sea level, and the South Island is more mountainous than the North. Coupled with mountains are hauntingly beautiful glacial lakes, some of which are more than 300 metres deep.

On the east coast there are wide, dry plains, across which braided rivers bring water from melted snow. To the west of the Southern Alps are rain forests, and on both sides of the mountains huge glaciers creak and groan in their frozen courses.

In Central Otago the autumn leaves each year turn a rich, burning gold, and everywhere are reminders of those who came in quest of metal of a similar hue. In the south-western corner, among the fiords and mountains that make up the Fiordland National Park, a sense of mystery and timelessness prevails.

New Zealand and its South Island are still young, vital and partly formed. For settlers there are still lands to claim; for travellers there are sights that retain an undiscovered air; and for everyone there are experiences to be had that attest to the uniqueness of Te Waka a Maui — the canoe of Maui.

1. A coastal scene near Punakaiki.

2. A Mount Gerald ski tour. Skiers can leave from and return to the ski area by plane.

2

1

2

3

1. Sometimes it is almost a millpond, but every so often the Roaring Forties help Cook Strait live up to its reputation as one of the roughest stretches of water in the world. The twenty-kilometre-wide gap between New Zealand's North and South Islands takes its name from the 18th-Century British explorer, Captain James Cook, who first charted its waters and experienced its unpredictable moods. Stocky, specially designed ferries, such as this one seen near the entrance to the South Island's Tory Channel, take about three hours and twenty minutes to make the crossing from Wellington in the North Island to Picton in the South.

2. 3. Tory Channel lies between Arapawa Island and the eastern finger of Queen Charlotte Sound

4

on the breathtaking ferry course through sheltered waters to Picton, the southern terminal. Early last century seamen in this area were always on the lookout for whales — a pursuit which lasted until 1964 when the whaling station at Whekenui Bay was closed. The channel is named after a survey vessel which sailed through on its way to Wellington in 1839.

4. The hulk of the *Edwin Fox* provides a lonely reminder of the past, while far across the glassy surface of Queen Charlotte Sound a ferry slides by. On 31 January 1770 Captain Cook went ashore from his barque *Endeavour* in Ship Cove, claimed the South Island for King George III and named the sound after the monarch's consort, Queen Charlotte Sophie.

1. Picton may be journey's end for the ferry crossing from Wellington, but each year it is the starting point for thousands of South Island holidays. It's also the beginning of the southern half of the main-trunk railway line and State Highway 1, which run down the eastern coast of the island. Snuggled deep in the folds of Queen Charlotte Sound, Picton offers the charms of serenity, magnificent fishing, spectacular scenery, delightful bush walks and a sense of history just made.

2. A timeless view of Queen Charlotte Sound from Grove Road. Perhaps it looked like this two centuries ago when a young botanist aboard the *Endeavour*, whose later knighthood made him Sir Joseph Banks, wrote in his journal: "I was awakened by the singing of the birds ashore, from whence we are distant not a quarter of a mile. They seemed to strain their throats with emulation, and made, perhaps, the most melodious wild music I have ever heard, almost emulating small bells, but with the most tunable silver sound imaginable."

3. Tuataras caused great consternation among naturalists in Europe last century when it was discovered they were not lizards, but living links with the reptiles that roamed the earth in the dim past. They are found mostly on New Zealand's offshore islands, and some about sixty centimetres long have been estimated to be 150 years old. (Some estimates have ranged up to 300 years because little is known about these remarkable reptiles.)

1

2

1. For those who want to bottle up part of their holiday and take it home to savour, the vineyards at Renwick are a recommended stopover. Renwick, situated about thirteen kilometres from the township of Blenheim in central Marlborough, has long been a market-gardening area. Now it is winning renown with grapes that produce wine to tickle the most discerning palates.

2. Best Nelson hops ripening in the sun.

3. Maitai Valley from Observation Point. Who would think that in this beautiful river valley anything as ghastly as ambush and murder could occur? But in 1866, on the Maungatapu walking track which passes through the area, a gang of highwaymen robbed and murdered five travellers. Nelson is only twelve kilometres away from the Maitai Valley, which offers views such as this from Observation Point.

1

2

1. With the tower of Nelson
Cathedral rising in the background,
sightseers and shoppers take time
out for afternoon tea at a roadside
café. Nelson is the centre of a rich
market-gardening area and enjoys
one of the highest annual sunshine
counts in New Zealand. It is the
home port of a busy fishing fleet
and a popular holiday and
retirement centre.

2. Beside the fruits of the soil,
Nelson is becoming famous for its
craft products. Sculptor Karl de
Smit is one of a lively group of
potters, artists and craftspeople
who find the atmosphere of the
district does wonders for their
work.

3. Suburbia, one hundred years
ago. Part of pioneer Nelson is
preserved in this row of practical
wooden houses right on the street
front.

4. In West Germany, Britain and
other Common Market countries —
not to mention the Middle East —
the arrival of a shipment of New
Zealand apples is delicious news.
The odds are they come from
Nelson, because with Hawke's Bay
in the North Island the district
competes for the title of Big Apple
in the industry. Between them the
two districts' export earnings are
well in excess of $100 million per
year.

3

4

1. Four boys, two bats and a
ball add up to a test match,
schoolboy-style in the farming
district of Moutere, to the west of
Nelson in Tasman Bay.

2. 3. Around the South Island coast
there are numerous bays and
inlets which make ideal places for
getting away from it all. Mapua
Inlet doesn't appear on many
maps, but it fits into this category
nicely. The Monarch butterfly, along
with the shags, herons and a
solitary gull are only some of the
many species found in this quiet
area.

4. A view of the wide expanse of
Tasman Bay from Ruby Bay, which
lies almost midway between
Nelson and Motueka.

3

1

2

1. 2. The Kaiteriteri Beach is a popular resort area near Motueka, on the western shores of Tasman Bay. It was visited in October 1841 by Captain Arthur Wakefield, the New Zealand Company's agent for the Nelson settlement. He inspected Kaiteriteri as a possible site for Nelson township, but eventually passed it over. Nevertheless, a memorial to Captain Wakefield and the Riwaka pioneers tells of the little bay's brush with fame.

3. Adrift in a river of sparkling glass, a power-boat explores the Falls River Inlet on the western shores of Tasman Bay. But although the scene looks peaceful enough, the river earns its name by dropping more than 1,000 metres in just ten kilometres.

4. A picturesque anchorage at Torrent Bay, on the north-western shore of Tasman Bay.

3

4

1

1. The Cobb Valley carves its way down mountains between the Peel and Lockett Ranges. Its path is marked by the Cobb River, which first flows through the reservoir of a hydro dam and then plunges to a meeting with the Takaka River and the ocean mid-way around the curve of Golden Bay at the north-western tip of the South Island. It is beautiful, rugged bush country.

2. The nature of the scenery in Golden Bay is very similar to that of the Cobb Valley, as this view from the coast road shows. The Dutch explorer Abel Tasman previously named this area Murderers' Bay in 1642 when four of his crew were killed by Maoris. D'Urville, another explorer, called it Massacre Bay, a name kept until 1842 when the discovery of coal at Takaka put Coal Bay on the map. That name disappeared in 1857 when hunters found gold in the Aorere River, resulting in yet another new name — however, this one seems destined to last.

3. A breakwater reaches out to sea at Pohara Beach, a popular holiday area in Golden Bay, nine kilometres north-east of the township of Takaka. In the distance is the Golden Bay cement works.

2

3

1

1. 2. Captain James Cook named this area Farewell Spit because it was the last part of New Zealand he saw as he set sail for Great Britain — and it has been the last piece of land seen from many a ship that has gone aground there. Visitors can drive down the twenty-four-kilometre-long spit at the north-western finger of the South Island. A lighthouse marks journey's end, and there's the added attraction of a refuge for tiny godwits which rest there in preparation for flights half-way around the world to Siberia.

2

3

3. The Takaka River saw its own brief period of gold fever in the 1850s, but now enjoys a quieter life as a tourist attraction. The region is rich in mineral deposits of various kinds and has a reputation as Marble Mountain Country, thanks to a rich seam of hard crystalline limestone.

4. Rotoiti means "small lake" in Maori, but these canoeists are enjoying one of a large range of activities available on or around this glacial lake. Boating, hiking, picnicking, swimming, hunting and skiing are all enjoyed in this part of the Nelson Lakes National Park.

4

1. 2. Once the rocky Kaikoura coastline was dotted with numerous Maori pa. Later, keen-eyed whalers waited there for their quarry to pass by. Captain Cook called the peninsula "Lookers On" after a group of Maoris in four double canoes paddled out to look at the *Endeavour*, but refused to come alongside. The peninsula itself is about 180 kilometres north of Christchurch and has a seal colony and reefs that have been designated a wildlife refuge.

3. Enjoying the wide-open spaces at Hanmer in North Canterbury. The region is best known for the Hanmer Springs spa and health resort, which has a world-wide reputation.

3

1

2

1. The braided pattern of many of the rivers draining the Canterbury Plains is evident in this view of the Waiau River from the Hanmer Bridge. There are five rivers of the same name in New Zealand, but this one is said in Maori legend to have once been a young girl who lived in the Spenser Mountains with her lover, Waiau-toa (the Clarence River). When the rivers are flushed with the spring thaw, the separated lovers are said to be weeping.

2. Ever since their discovery in 1859, the Hanmer Springs, with their soft and soothing waters, have drawn people seeking treatment and relaxation. Farming,

forestry, tourism, and skiing at nearby Amuri have ensured the region's prosperity.

3. Trees at Hamner on a frosty morning.

4. The 150-kilometre-long Waimakariri River rises in the glaciers of the Southern Alps, breaks free of the rocks and crags and then sprawls its way across the Canterbury Plains to the sea. Wreathed in winter mists, it leaves no doubt that its name was well chosen! Waimakariri means "cold water".

3

4

1. The snow-capped Southern Alps provide the frosting on the horizon in this view of Christchurch city. Sometimes the climate of the alps reaches out to the city and helps create the greatest range of temperatures of any of the main centres. The mean daily minimum in winter (July) is 1°C and the mean summer daily maximum (January) is 22°C. However, gusty föhn winds descending from the alps can send temperatures soaring to over 35°C in summer.

2. Christchurch, the largest city in the South Island, derives much of its distinctive English atmosphere from the River Avon which flows through Hagley Park en route to the sea. However, the name has Scottish rather than English origins. The original sketch map of the settlement shows it as "the River Shakespeare", but it was later renamed after a stream near Riccarton, Kilmarnock, County Ayrshire, in south-west Scotland.

3. Christchurch had its beginnings in an orderly reconstruction of the way of life many of its settlers had left behind. There are constant reminders of "The Old Country" in many of its buildings and place names. The houses in Durham Street are such a reminder and are becoming much sought after.

4. The Chamber of Commerce building is another with a familiar look about it. Peering over its brick shoulders is a relative newcomer, Noah's Hotel.

5. Like a brace of misty lollipops, the twin sprays of the Ferrier Fountain give a softening touch to the walls of the Christchurch Town Hall. The complex, opened in 1972, includes the James Hay theatre, which seats more than 1,000 people; an oval-shaped auditorium seating another 2,660; the Limes Room for banquets, balls and other functions; a restaurant and public concourse areas. The Town Hall was the venue for some of the activities of the Commonwealth Games in 1974.

2

3

4

1. As early as 1864 the people of Christchurch set about building their cathedral, which now dominates Cathedral Square in the centre of the city. However, the construction was beset with problems due to difficult economic times. The nave was not ready for use until 1881, and the transepts and chancel were opened in 1904. The Gothic-style building is said to have been modelled on that of Caen Cathedral in Normandy.

2. Lancaster Park is known to rugby and cricket fans the world over as an arena where history has been made and sporting heroics have inspired legends. However, it has seen much more than cricket and rugby. Olympic runner Peter Snell set two world records there, and soccer, rugby league, tennis and even swimming have had their great moments on or near the hallowed turf.

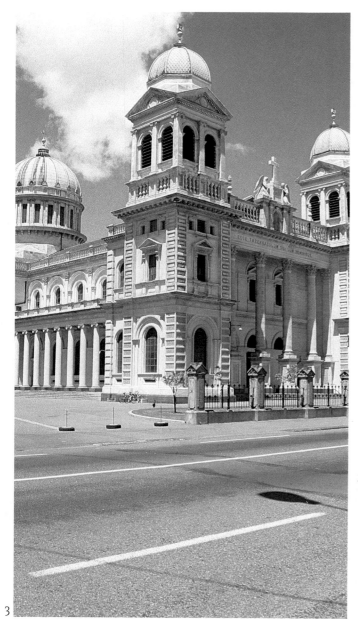

3

4

3. The Roman Catholic Basilica, the Cathedral of the Blessed Sacrament, is holy ground of a more traditional kind. This imposing Roman Renaissance-style building in Barbadoes Street was designed by Francis William Petre.

4. Inside it is even more impressive with its massive dome above the altar and an air of space and graciousness.

1

2

3

4

1, 2. The gardens and parks of Christchurch are a constant delight, but chief among them is Hagley Park, which would be the envy of much larger cities around the world. The 200-hectare park was named after the family estate of the Fourth Baron Lyttelton, who was chairman of the Canterbury Association in 1849. It includes numerous sports grounds, the city's Botanic Gardens, a golf course and several specialty gardens. On the eastern side of the park is the Canterbury Museum, which houses one of the finest ornithological collections in the Southern Hemisphere, and many fine pioneer displays.

3. Looking at Christchurch today it is difficult to believe it ever passed through a rough-and-ready pioneer stage. Everything seems too well planned and orderly, right down to the neatly-clipped grass for the polo ponies. The Town Hall underlines the Christchurch citizen's love of culture, but sport has also been strong from the early days — especially those activities favoured by the English.

4. "The Golden Half-Mile" at Brighton is one of the busiest shopping centres in Christchurch.

1

1. A searchlight mirror provides
a lot of fun in its second life at the
Ferrymead Historic Park,
Christchurch.

2. Lyttelton Harbour — a quiet
anchorage for yachts and other
pleasure craft.

2

1. This immigrant, who received VIP treatment all the way to Orana Park at Christchurch, gets plenty of callers each day and treats them with regal indifference.

2. Sumner Beach, a pleasant retreat just 11 kilometres from the centre of Christchurch.

3. Looking towards Little River from Lake Forsyth, Banks Peninsula.

4. Akaroa Harbour.

3

4

1. A baton change for relay racers on Summit Road in the Port Hills, Christchurch, as they pound their way towards Akaroa.

2. The settlement of Akaroa, nestling in its sheltered harbour, was once a base for whalers and could easily have become another French territory in the South Pacific. In 1838, Jean Langlois, the master of the *Cachalot*, negotiated with the local Maori people to buy the whole of Banks Peninsula. He made a downpayment and returned to France to arrange a company of settlers. Before they arrived, the Treaty of Waitangi had been signed, making New Zealand a colony of Great Britain.

1

2

1. Governor Hobson assured the French that their property would be respected, but to make his position clear he sent Captain Owen Stanley in HMS *Britomart* to hoist the British flag at Akaroa. A monument at Green's Point marks the site where this was accomplished on 11 August 1840. Another reminder is one of the *Britomart's* guns mounted in a park setting overlooking the harbour.

2. Dinghies provide a splash of colour on Akaroa's waterfront.

3

3. An old try-pot, providing mute
testimony to the endeavours of
whalers in the Akaroa area.

4. Langlois-Enteveneaux House,
with French street signs outside,
firmly establishes the French
presence in its role as a museum.
Rue Lavaud honours the captain of
L'Aube, a French naval corvette,
which accompanied Langlois' party
of settlers aboard the *Comte de
Paris*.

4

1. Part rogue, part robber, part clown — the kea will remove anything from a camp site that isn't tied down, and he will entertain you with his antics as he does so. The hooked beak reveals that he is a bird of prey, and some high country farmers would call him killer as well, blaming him for vicious attacks on sheep. That apart, the kea is sure to charm visitors to the South Island's high-country regions.

2. When naturalist Sir Joseph Banks wrote in 1770 of waking to the sound of beautiful bird song like small silver bells, one of the culprits probably was what is now called a bellbird. To ornithologists this forest mimic is known as *Anthornis melanura*, and the Maori people have assigned the more melodic name of korimako.

3. A precarious-looking road cuts through the formidable Otira Gorge, connecting Westland and Canterbury. In pioneer times, stage coaches rattled back and forth regularly, keeping open this important route for passengers and commerce. The eight-and-a-half-kilometre Otira railway tunnel brought new ease to the journey.

4. Magnificent native bush dominates the scenery on the Heaphy Track, which links Bainham in Golden Bay and Karamea on the West Coast. Trampers usually allow four to six days for the journey.

1. Even the highway over Karamea Bluff is lined with bush.

2. When the first batch of assisted immigrants sponsored by the Nelson Provincial Government moved into the Karamea area in 1874, they had high hopes for a prosperous future. However, nature treated them unkindly and many walked off their properties, discouraged by the bush and clay soil. Some who battled on gave up after the severe Murchison earthquake wrecked the district's port and roads in 1929. The descendants of those who stayed now reap the benefits.

3. Often the West Coast highway swings close to the surf and hugs the shoreline around abrupt headlands, such as these near Punakaiki, a farming district forty-two kilometres north of Greymouth.

4. In a different mood, much of the West Coast is still as wild and mysterious as it was in the times of New Zealand's early explorers.

3

4

1

3. On the site of an old goldfield, enterprising West Coasters have erected Shantytown, a life-sized replica of a New Zealand frontier town. There visitors can walk the streets of a mining town of the 1880s, browse through 19th-Century shops or ride behind the ancient locomotive, Kaitangata, to a gold claim where they can try their luck. Shantytown is located at Rutherglen, ten kilometres south of Greymouth.

4. The fishing fleet at Greymouth, the West Coast's chief commercial centre.

2

3

1, 2. Certainly not like mother used to make, the Punakaiki pancakes are actually fluted limestone rocks, carved by the rushing surf and fierce blowholes in the area. The display is accompanied by awesome rumblings and boomings as the sea continues its sculpting. The Pancake Rocks are situated to the south of Punakaiki township, near the mouth of the Punakaiki River.

5. Lake Kaniere from the eastern shore. The lake, situated approx. 18 km from Hokitika, frequently provides visitors with superb reflections. It is a favourite for waterskiers, swimmers, picnickers and fishermen.

4

5

1. The Lake Kaniere area in a
misty mood.

2. The Heaphy Track, regarded
as one of the country's most
spectacular walks, bursts out
to a magnificent sweep of
isolated, sandy coastline
at Scotts Beach.

presented to King George V as a Coronation gift and was melted down for a tea service.

3. Don't expect to have the road to yourself on the West Coast — the livestock are often going places, too. This motor-cycle sheep-herder is plying his trade near Harihari in South Westland.

1, 2. Who knows how much more gold the Westland bush conceals? "Not much", old-timers might say as they watch travellers motor by on the sealed highway near Ross. But it doesn't stop them talking about "the Honourable Roddy", a 2,807-gram nugget found near the township in 1903 by John Scott and Arthur Sharp. It was later

1. Although Lake Matheson was an afterthought of the Fox Glacier, it is high on the list of priorities for tourists, particularly photographers who make much of the beautiful reflections of distant mountains. As the glacier retreated, it left an isolated pocket of ice behind in a depression. When the ice melted, Lake Matheson was born.

2. Most people go to the beach to fish or swim, but in April 1866 James Edwin Gillespie found gold here. The Westland beach that now bears his name looks less than inviting here, but it soon supported a busy mining operation, signs of which can still be seen.

3. The massive Southern Alps have produced some of the biggest glaciers outside the Himalayas and polar regions. However, here the Fox Glacier seems small far in the distance, its blue-white expanse blending with the early-morning sky and clouds.

3. Snowfields surrounding the fifteen-kilometre-long Fox Glacier help to conceal treacherous crevasses as it makes its majestic descent from just over 2,700 metres above sea level to only 245 metres. The Fox Glacier township at the edge of the river flat below the glacier is a popular and well-equipped tourist resort. The glacier had royal beginnings, first being named after Prince Alfred (Queen Victoria's second son) and then "Prince Albert" after the Queen's consort. The final "Fox" honours Sir William Fox, who was four times Prime Minister of New Zealand.

4. Fishing boats shelter in the calm waters of Jackson Bay, a Westland fishing port south of the Haast River.

5. A glimpse of Lake Moeraki which lies on the coast north of Haast.

1. Keeping a wary eye on passers-by along a bush path is a wood pigeon, or Kereru. Once a popular gamebird of the Maori, it is now protected.

2. The Minehaha bush walk is one of several interesting hikes that may be made in the glacier area.

3

4

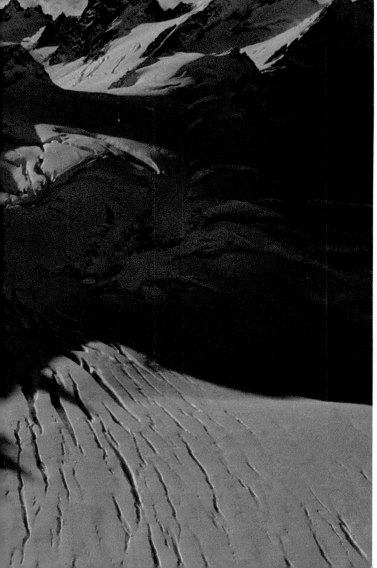

5

2

1. In all of the Southern Alps Mount Tasman is second only to Mount Cook. Named after the Dutch explorer who was the first of the European wanderers to discover New Zealand, Mount Tasman reaches 3,498 metres skyward, offering a constant challenge to climbers.

2. Skiers come from all over the world to enjoy the snow at Mount Hutt, which rises from the Canterbury Plains 108 kilometres south-west of Christchurch. Part of its popularity is due to its relative closeness to the city of Christchurch, and part to the long skiing season, which extends from May till October.

3. From its pastures New Zealand earns 75 per cent of its overseas income. Sheep outnumber humans more than twenty to one, and New Zealand ranks in the top three trading nations for most agricultural products. This field of clover is near Prebbleton, a township thirteen kilometres south-west of Christchurch.

3

1. Evening begins to cast its shadows over farmland at Fairlie in South Canterbury. The district was given its name by early settlers because of its resemblance to Fairlie in Strathclyde, Western Scotland.

2. Bob Anderson discusses some of the features of the Rodgers engine he restored after it was recovered from the Oreti River in Southland. The engine hauled the first Christchurch-Dunedin express and, as the original "Kingston Flyer", earned fame in the Queenstown area. A love for things of the past is particularly strong in the south.

3

3. Few churches in New Zealand are as much photographed or beloved to photographers as the Church of the Good Shepherd at Lake Tekapo in South Canterbury. The lake covers eighty-three square kilometres and is tucked into the eastern fringe of the Southern Alps. The simple stone church was built in 1935 as a memorial to the pioneer runholders of the Mackenzie Country, as the high-country grasslands are known.

4. There is no need for stained glass with windows like these. This view of the lake is from inside the church, looking out over the altar.

4

1

2

1. At the best of times the water of the lake is rather cold for swimming, but in winter Lake Tekapo's garb echoes its glacial birth.

2. Lake Pukaki, a near neighbour of Tekapo. The cool, blue water and its icy surrounds impersonate the mountains and sky. The reflection is so crisp you may have to mark the tops and bottoms of your photographs to avoid displaying them upside down by mistake. Like Tekapo, Lake Pukaki is of glacial origin and contributes water to hydro-electric power schemes.

3. Mount Cook towers above the placid waters of Lake Pukaki.

4. Mount Cook's Maori name is Aorangi, or cloud piercer, and it dominates the tourist resort area at its base in the Mount Cook National Park. The scenic beauty and range of alpine activities bring tourists and climbers from all over the world.

3

4

1. Mount Cook, with dawn etching out the three peaks covered by climbers attempting the grand traverse.

3. Ski-plane flights around the Mount Cook region cram days of sight-seeing into a few minutes. The sensation is one of being surrounded by expanse after expanse of snow-covered peaks and valleys. For a climax the plane may land on a snowfield high in the mountains. Mount Cook in the background is, at 3,764 metres, New Zealand's highest peak.

2. The Mount Cook lily (*Ranunculus lyalli*), actually a mountain buttercup, is probably the most familiar of New Zealand alpine flowers. For those who rarely visit Mount Cook, the lily is recognised on aircraft and buses as the symbol of Mount Cook Airlines.

4. The Hermitage, a famous tourist hotel in Mount Cook Village, has been the starting point for many expeditions. Sir Edmund Hillary, the New Zealander who became the first man to climb Mount Everest, did much of his early mountaineering in the Mount Cook National Park.

5. A solitary alpine hut perched on the Tasman Saddle.

1

2

3

4

1. Easy ski slopes lead down to the gigantic and other-worldly Tasman Glacier — a twenty-nine kilometre staircase which descends to the valley floor. It is the largest glacier in New Zealand and one of the longest found in a temperate zone. The glacier and the river that emerges from beneath it were named after the explorer Abel Tasman.

2. Tinged with pink early-morning light, Mount Sefton (3,157 metres) greets a new day from this vantage point overlooking the confluence of the Hooker and Mueller Glaciers near Mount Cook.

3. The Ohau Range to the west of Lake Ohau forms the boundary between the Mackenzie County in South Canterbury and the Waitaki County in Central Otago. A skifield for advanced and intermediate skiers looks out over the lake below.

4, 5. The Lindis Pass in summer, and dressed for winter. An Otago surveyor, John Turnbull Thompson, discovered the pass in December 1857 and named it after the holy island of Lindisfarne off the coast of Northumberland, in north-east England. A monument on the pass marks the point where red deer were released in 1871. In the absence of natural predators, the deer flourished.

5

1

2

1. The spreading green of a lucerne farm at Luggate, near Wanaka. In the gold-rush era, farmlands further north produced wheat which was milled at Luggate and found a ready market with the miners.

2. When miners and settlers first moved into Central Otago they used the ever-present stone as a building material. Often the shacks, outbuildings and walls they constructed so cleverly were erected without the use of mortar. Examples of such work can be found at Bendigo on the eastern banks of the Clutha River.

3. Sheep graze on the fertile
Clutha Valley river flats near Tarras
in Central Otago.

3

1. The annual blossom festival each September at Alexandra, Central Otago, is a time of thanksgiving and goodwill for this rich farming land near the junction of the Clutha and Manuherikia Rivers. People come for many miles to see the parade and join in the festivities.

2. A shepherd, aided by his dogs, moves sheep between paddocks lined by lupins.

3 ,4. Everywhere at St Bathans are signs of the miners who came, struggled for gold and left when the supply dwindled. One of the few buildings on the old main street still in good repair is the Vulcan Hotel, which dates from 1869. Blue Lake, a crater 800 metres long and more than fifty metres deep, is the result of a massive excavation by miners, and is now filled with water. In winter it freezes over to provide an excellent rink for skating and curling.

4

1. It is easy to assume Waimate was always like this, but the township had its beginning only last century in a meeting between two men in 1854. A settler, Michael Studholme, and a Maori chief, Te Huruhuru, negotiated the sale of the land somewhere near the end of this avenue.

2. The nature of the land changes from mountains to the plains of South Canterbury near Waimate, with stooks of hay in the foreground and the shadows of the Hunter Hills beyond.

3

3. The Roman Catholic basilica in Timaru dates back to 1910 and shows that the people of the day enjoyed the sense of permanence created by imposing buildings in brick and stone. Timaru, the centre of South Canterbury, celebrated its centenary in 1968.

4. Approaching squall near Oamaru.

4

1

2

3

4

1. There is a richness about the land and its colours that marks the south as a special place. Something of this quality shows here in this view from the Haast Highway near Makaroa.

2. Lovely enough to be the subject of an oil painting, Lake Wanaka parallels Lake Hawea on the other side of the road leading to the Haast. Although it is forty-five kilometres long. Lake Wanaka is only six kilometres across at its widest point — a clue to its glacial origin. While elsewhere in Otago others were looking for gold, settlers around Wanaka established huge sheep stations and made their fortunes from wool and lamb.

3. In places Lake Wanaka is more than 300 metres deep, but most people see only the limpid surface before brilliant surrounding foliage steals their eyes away.

4. Delicate fronds of toe-toe curve with the wind against a backdrop of 3,027-metre Mount Aspiring near the southern reaches of the Southern Alps. Mount Aspiring, which in some respects has been likened to the Matterhorn in Switzerland, forms a natural boundary between the lakes of Central Otago and the rain forests of Westland.

1. Miners came and went, but the farmers stayed. That's the story of the beautiful Cardrona Valley, named by a Scotsman, Robert Wilkin, the first runholder in the Wanaka region. Cardrona lies on the eyecatching route between Lake Wanaka and Queenstown — the highest highway in New Zealand.

2. During the height of the gold rush, Cardrona's population reached 5,000, and saloons such as the historic Cardrona Hotel did a roaring trade. Sometimes there was a bit too much roaring, and the trade was in punches. Storekeepers and publicans often used their own security forces to preserve the peace.

3. This pioneer cottage is in a street of cottages in the centre of Arrowtown, on the banks of the Arrow River. These days the most obvious gold gleams from the branches of the trees that arch over the main street. A must for visitors, whether in search of gold or history, is a visit to the Lake County Museum where the region's past is most commendably preserved.

4. When beautiful Lake Hayes was named after its discoverer, an Australian stockman named Donald Hay, his name was misspelled. What is more, when Hay arrived in Dunedin to apply for lakeside pasture land, he found the news had preceded him and a claim had been lodged by an employee of the Lands and Survey office. Lake Hayes is situated between Queenstown and Arrowtown, and is renowned for its excellent fishing.

1. In 1863 a public meeting at a small settlement on the shores of Lake Wakatipu decided the township site was fit for a queen — so they called it Queenstown. Now it is one of the major tourist areas of New Zealand, and among its attractions features a cableway to a restaurant at the top of Bob's Peak. The awesome view of the lake and surrounding countryside is guaranteed to sharpen any appetite for more of what the region has to offer.

2. Paddles ply the water in unison as canoeists head out across the Frankton arm of Lake Wakatipu. The mountain range in the background was named The Remarkables by a pioneer Otago surveyor, Alexander Garvie, in 1857. Covering some 291 square kilometres, Wakatipu is the longest lake in the South Island and the third largest in New Zealand. Every five minutes or so the lake level rises and falls as much as twelve centimetres, a phenomenon scientists say is due to either wind or variations in atmospheric pressure. Maori legend has it that the pulsing is caused by the heart of a deposed giant.

3 — 5. In winter The Remarkables range is covered in snow; in summer it stands as gaunt, baked stone, with remarkable presence. The highest point is Double Cone, which reaches 2,343 metres. The extremely rugged nature of The Remarkables gives the range a grandeur missing from other more gently moulded mountains.

6. Waterlilies, Queenstown.

3 — 5

6

1. Hundreds of prospectors swarmed to the Arrow River in the 1860s after a share of the significant amounts of gold that were taken out of what is sometimes regarded as little more than a mountain stream. Fossickers and holiday-makers still try their luck with pan and shovel, and are often rewarded with traces of colour.

2. Hell's Gate is an appropriate introduction to what lies beyond in Skippers Canyon. The "gate" is one of many awesome features of the thirty-two kilometres of scary road, track and cliffside ledge that have been chipped through this gorge near Queenstown. While not for the faint-hearted, it has provided a popular day-trip for tourists.

3. "Skippers", as it is often called, is said to have been named after a ship's captain whose vessel was wrecked near the Otago Heads. The Skipper, as he was known to all, made his way to Queenstown and discovered gold in the gorge in the 1860s. A dredge worked these waters as recently as the 1930s.

4. Winding up the Shotover River at seventy kilometres/hour in a jetboat is the highlight of many southern holidays. In spite of the speed of the boats — a New Zealand invention — and the rugged nature of the surroundings, the thrills are as safe as a fairground ride.

When summer goes,
Queenstown barely misses a beat.
Winter tourists arrive in their
thousands to pit themselves
against the ski slopes of Coronet
Peak. The facilities are excellent
and include instruction for
beginners. Ski lifts and tows
provide easy access to the
best snow and make it possible
for skiers to spend all day on
slopes of their choice. Although
they had been used by local skiers
since the early days of this
century, the fields were first
developed by members of the
Wigley family after they flew over
the area and realised its potential.

1. With her smart, red funnel towering high above boarding passengers, the S.S. *Earnslaw* prepares to make yet another cruise on Lake Wakatipu. She made her debut soon after the Railways Department purchased all privately owned service shipping on the lake in 1911, and proceeded to win hearts by the thousand. Fifty years later the *Earnslaw* was a legend, but roads and road transport had improved enormously and provided too much competition for the ferry. In 1968, the Railways Department decided to scrap her.

2. Luckily, the public outcry that greeted the announcement forced a change of heart and the *Earnslaw*, now under private ownership, still carries passengers across the lake. There are faster ways to travel, but none would dispute that the *Earnslaw* is something special.

3. The Kawarau River makes its exit from Lake Wakatipu on the Frankton Arm.

2

3

1

2

3

1. Farming, which began in Arrowtown when the gold started to run out, is still thriving.

2. You are welcome to come hunting — with cameras, not guns — at Deer Park Heights near Queenstown. Here, in their natural habitat, it is possible to see deer, chamois, thar and other alpine animals at their best.

3. The head of Lake Wakatipu and Mount Earnslaw as seen from Glenorchy, the starting point for tramping trips and climbing trips in the Rees Valley and neighbouring mountains.

4. Trampers arrive at the start of the forty-kilometre Routeburn Track. The three-to-four-day hike links the Queenstown region with Fiordland. Trampers traverse the southern reaches of the Southern Alps, passing through Mount Aspiring and Fiordland National Parks.

5. In pre-European times and perhaps as recently as 1852, the Maori people used the Routeburn track to get access to West Coast greenstone and preserve trading links with villages in South Westland. Today a sense of adventure prevails for all who make the trek through these valleys, mountains and forest paths.

6. A silver fern is New Zealand's national emblem. This, and ferns of many other types, may be seen all along the track.

4

5

6

1

2

1. The Moeraki Boulders have puzzled people for generations — they lie upon the east-coast beach like giant marbles abandoned by giant children. A Maori legend says they are the petrified remains of seed kumara and cargo washed ashore from a capsized canoe; however, the scientific explanation is more prosaic. They are septarian concretions formed millions of years ago by the accumulation of limestone salts on the sea floor. They can be seen between the fishing village of Moeraki and the township of Hampden.

2,3. The tidal flats of Otago Peninsula are teeming with life, ranging from tiny sea creatures to the majestic Royal Albatross with a wing-span of up to three-and-a-half metres. Penguins, gulls and wading birds fuss around the crags, and shags bob about in search of prey. The Royal Albatross colony on Taiaroa Head falls within the boundary of Dunedin City, and is the only one in the world so close to civilisation.

4. Looking north from Waitati towards Blueskin Bay.

1

2

3

fascinating collection of relics from whaling and mining days, early paintings and photographs, diaries, furniture and farm equipment. The displays are rated among the best in the Southern Hemisphere.

5. Dunedin's Law Courts present a facade of elaborate stonework.

4

1. The gold rush helped make Dunedin the business centre of New Zealand in the late 19th Century. This is still demonstrated today by the stately homes of merchant princes of yester-year — among them two castles. The city now takes pride in its many fine gardens and homes, some of which are open to the public.

2. George Street to the north and Princes Street to the south are the main thoroughfares in Dunedin City. They meet at the Octagon from where all commercial life radiates under the watchful eyes of a statue of Robbie Burns. Many of the churches cluster around the Octagon as well.

3. Dunedin was founded in 1848 as a Free Church of Scotland settlement, and the Presbyterian influence has always been strong in spite of the pot-pourri of races originally attracted by the search for gold. The present First Church was built in a Gothic Revivalist style and dates from 1873. Local hard, grey stone was used for the base and walls, while the decorative touches were wrought from some of the finest Oamaru stone ever quarried.

4. This cable car has its last resting place in the Otago Early Settlers Association Museum and Portrait Gallery in Dunedin. It is in good company among a

5

1

1. Despite its beauty and size, Lake Te Anau works for a living. Some of the water from this, the largest South Island lake, discharges into the Waiau River which flows into Lake Manapouri and helps feed the massive Manapouri hydro-electric project. There are enough activities available on and around the lake to keep visitors busy for many days, among them the world-famous Milford Track walk, which begins at Glade House.

2. The Eglinton valley provides entry to Fiordland National Park from Te Anau, offering incomparable scenery along the way.

1. Perhaps the most easily-recognised feature of Milford Sound is Mitre Peak, which spears upward for 1,692 metres to become one of the world's highest mountains rising directly from the sea. Its name was bestowed upon it because of the peak's resemblance to a bishop's headgear.

2. An "Islander" lands at the Milford Sound airstrip, which provides the speediest link with the outside world. Sometimes this is the only link as storms can cut off the highway leading to the Milford resort area.

3. Sudden weather changes are common in Milford Sound and along the Milford Track, "the finest walk in the world". Here the forbidding outline of Mitre Peak is a reminder to climbers that it is not to be taken lightly.

1

1. When mountains are coupled with a steady rainfall, the result is high waterfalls, with which Milford Sound abounds. The Bowen Falls drop in two stages for 160 metres en route from the Bowen River to Milford Sound. They are named after a 19th-Century governor of New Zealand, Sir George Ferguson Bowen.

2. "As idle as a painted ship upon a painted ocean ..." Usually anything but idle, this yacht called in at Milford Sound from Auckland during a circumnavigation of New Zealand.

3. The northern side of Milford Sound is dominated by Mount Pembroke (2,045 metres), which looms above the Palisades ridge. It is thought that Mount Pembroke was given its name by John Grono, a pioneer Welsh sealer, in memory of the town of Pembroke in his home country.

2

1. Large cruise ships often enter Milford Sound and anchor at Harrison Cove. Although its attractiveness would justify a stopover, the cove is the only suitable anchorage in the area.

2. Rudyard Kipling called Milford Sound the eighth wonder of the world. The Nobel Prize-winning author chose his words carefully, and few would argue that the sound, a true Norwegian-style fiord, does not deserve such praise. The approach from the sea shows the sheerness of its glacially-carved walls, and the inner reaches are deeper than the entrance. The entrance-way is an invitation to adventurers everywhere.

3. The Chasm, where the roaring Cleddau River has carved its way through solid rock near the road to Milford.

1

2

1. For many years the
Sutherland Falls were thought to
be the highest in the world. Now
they are ranked number five, but
they still rate as a heart-stopping
spectacle as they plunge in three
great leaps from Lake Quill in the
sky to the valley of the Arthur
River. They were discovered on 10
November 1880 by Scotsman
Donald Sutherland. The three
stages drop in turn 248 metres,
229 metres and 103 metres.

2. A walker on the Milford Track,
which stretches from the head of
Lake Te Anau to Milford Sound.

3. Yet another spectacle among the myriad waterfalls which seam the cliffs and mountainsides of Fiordland: this is Gate Pa Falls on the Milford Track.

4. The scenic Arthur River framed by bush.

1. A basket of wriggling, pink crays, which take on a distinctive orange hue when cooked.

2. Crayfishermen at work in the lonely waters of Fiordland. Their catch could grace tables in New Zealand, or in North America as rock lobster.

3. Milford Sound offers a bewildering array of breathtaking subjects for artists, such as this summer mountain scene.

4. In the Murchison Mountains near Te Anau, ornithologists made a startling discovery. One of New Zealand's flightless birds, the Takahe (*Notornis mantelli*) was thought to have joined the Moa in extinction, but in November 1948 a small colony was discovered. The Murchison Mountains are now a specially protected wilderness area to ensure the Takahe's survival.

5. A green parakeet, an Australian visitor that stayed to add its attractions to those of Milford Sound.

1

2

3

1. Coal trucks rumble through the snow from the Southland mining town of Nightcaps. The locality takes its name from that given to strange, conical hills nearby, which resemble night-time headgear. The deep south is one of the few areas of generally temperate New Zealand where snow falls outside the mountain ranges.

2. This imposing memorial to the Boer War stands in Invercargill, New Zealand's most southern city and certainly the most distant corner of the British Empire to respond to the call to arms in the South African conflict.

3. The colourful bricks and striking design of the First (Presbyterian) Church, Invercargill, have made it a landmark in the city since 1915. There are surprises inside, too, such as a sculptured wood panel of the Last Supper which was purchased in Venice by a pioneer pastor, Thomas Spencer Forsaith.

4. Raking leaves in Queens Park, an eighty-hectare reserve in the centre of Invercargill. This showplace of the city has had an interesting past, including time as a racecourse and sportsground. Now great care has been taken to develop an outstanding array of floral delights, a wildlife sanctuary, an aviary and a children's park.

5. Strollers enjoy a golden autumn avenue within the park.

Each year the nation's gourmets cast anxious glances south and wonder how the Bluff oyster catch is faring. Bluff is situated near the end of a peninsula which reaches out into Foveaux Strait between the South Island and Stewart Island. The surrounding waters abound with fish, among which the famed Bluff oysters hold a place of honour.

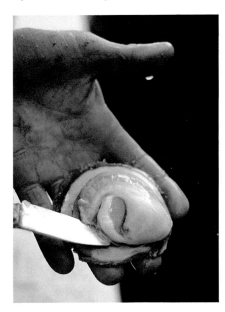

1

2

1. According to Maori legend, the North Island was a fish caught by the demi-god Maui from his canoe, the South Island. Some thirty kilometres south of the canoe is Stewart Island, said to be its anchor stone. When Captain James Cook sighted it, he wasn't sure whether he was seeing an island or a peninsula, so he cautiously named it South Cape. The principal settlement is Oban in Halfmoon Bay, where small craft abound.

2. Halfmoon Bay is where many of the bush walks and cruises to neighbouring islands begin.

3. The deeply indented coastline of Stewart Island gives it great scenic beauty.

4. Golden Bay, a cove on Paterson Inlet, a kilometre to the south-west, is also a good place for messing about in boats.

Dawn at Halfmoon Bay.